I dedicate this book to those whose support and encouragement set sail the vessel of my words. Thank you for igniting the torch of inspiration. You truly are the compass points of this poetic journey.

Kirsten Westholter

WHISPERS OF THE HEART

AUSTIN MACAULEY PUBLISHERS®

LONDON * CAMBRIDGE * NEW YORK * SHARJAH

ISBN - 9789948731030 - (Paperback)
ISBN - 9789948731047 - (E-Book)

Application Number: MC-10-01-7645271
Age Classification: E

The age group that matches the content of the books has been classified according to the age classification system issued by the UAE Media Council.

First Published 2024
AUSTIN MACAULEY PUBLISHERS FZE
Sharjah Publishing City
P.O Box [519201]
Sharjah, UAE
www.austinmacauley.ae
+971 655 95 202

I am deeply grateful to my muse, life with all its beauty and challenges, for fueling the poems that fill these pages. A huge thank you goes to my dear friends for their unwavering belief in me, as well as to the readers who hopefully find solace or resonance in my verses.

Table of Content

Foreword:
Rising from the Ashes

I've discovered a sacred space, a place where I transcend the boundaries of everyday life and give voice to my soul's depths. Presenting this collection of poems brings me both joy and vulnerability as it bears witness to my journey.

Professionally, I thrive as a Senior Culture and Leadership Transformation Advisor, dedicated to offering innovative solutions for businesses facing their toughest challenges. But beyond the boardrooms and strategic endeavors lies a hidden flame—a passion for poetry—that burns brightly within me.

My path led me from the comforts of Amsterdam to the vibrant landscapes of Dubai, leaving behind the familiarity and predictability of my previous life. It was a bold step into the unknown, forever altering the course of my existence. Inspiring others to step outside their comfort zones, ignite their inner fires, and follow their hearts has unveiled my own purpose.

The legend of the Phoenix intertwines with my story. Embracing the symbolism of rebirth and resilience, I've taken on the pseudonym Dubai Phoenix to honor the transformative power of rising from the ashes. Through my poetry, I strive to capture love's essence, the broad spectrum of emotions, and the sometimes uncomfortable truths within ourselves.

Every poem within these pages bears witness to my personal experiences and keen observations of the world. Themes of love, loss, and the Phoenix's profound journey are

"

interwoven, inviting exploration of the human spirit's intricacies and our shared emotions.

As you delve into this poetic collection, I invite you to join me on a profound exploration of the human condition. Let's embrace life's transformative nature and the power of choice. In every moment, we hold the potential to rise, reinvent ourselves, and create defining memories.

May my words ignite a fire within you, urging you beyond comfort zones, encouraging you to follow your heart's whispers, and boldly pursue your dreams. Through this poetic journey, may you find solace, inspiration, and the unwavering courage to rise from the ashes, embracing boundless possibilities.

With love and gratitude,
Kirsten, aka Dubai Phoenix

Of Passion and Romance

No Regrets, Only Memories

As the sun greets the horizon,
He fades from my dreams.
Did I summon him from deep within,
A creation of my own imagination?

Whispering softly, he declared,
"No regrets, only memories."
His kiss, a balm for my pain,
Tears brushed away, gently.

Free spirits, they say, do not weep,
Yet tears flow in tender release.
Embracing emotions, unburdened,
Strength found in vulnerability.

As the first light of dawn awakens me,
In that space between dreams and reality,
I find myself unsure of the borders,
Yet confident that all will be well.

With open arms, I'll embrace
The unknown that lies ahead.
For in memories, I find solace,
No regrets, only the echoes of time.

Skin Hunger

I love your eyes when they sparkle,
There is something hidden there,
A wild desire.
I love that special feeling when my nails
Cause shivers up your spine.
I love your hands when their touch
Sets my skin on fire.
I love how I forget to breathe
When your mouth whispers my name.

No colorless life, not for us,
Only excitement and adventures.
There is so much to explore.
No claiming, no jealousy,
Only trust and confidence.
That is when magic happens
Between you and me.

The world is shaking,
My mind is accelerating,
Adrenaline pumping.

Offer me your hunger,
I will offer you mine.
Predator and prey,
Prey and predator.

Skin hunger,
Skin hunger,
You,
Me.

Sunrise or Sunset

You are not my sunrise lover,
You are not a 8am
Sunrise.
The new day ignites my fire,
Tracing my fingertips
Along your skin.
My face pressed against your chest,
Your heart beating under my cheeks.
And you… you pretend
You are asleep.
Coffee is what you need.

You are not my sunrise lover,
You are a 7pm
Sunset.
Blossoming red and gold,
Caressing my body,
Blood rushing in our lips,
My hunger finally satisfied,
Your hands resting next to mine.

Does it really matter,
Sunrise or sunset,
Dawn or dusk,
Coffee or wine?

Of Desire and Passion

I love your eyes,
Lit with a passionate fire.
I want to be in your arms,
Where you hold me tight,
Safe from the outside world.
Never let me go.

I love your lips,
Whispering softly in my ear.
Strong women need that too.
Your kisses, my drug,
A wild desire.
The fire feels warm.
I am slightly out of control.

I don't want ordinary love.
I want the madness,
Leaving my head spinning.
Not the cold, calm kiss,
Nor the heart of a colorless bird.

Give me the love that is free,
No boundaries.
Kiss me today as if
Tomorrow does not exist.

There is only now,
A rollercoaster ride,
Over and over again.

Midnight Sky

As you stare into the sky,
Shining stars so bright,
Would you kiss the moon?
Will you fly above the cloud,
Like a majestic eagle,
With your wings stretched wide,
High above the earth,
Into the heavens.
Pilots feel closer to such a bird
Than any of us sitting in our seats.

What could you want more?
Sight grows sharper with distance.
Your gaze fixed on her,
Who shines above.
Love that never fades.
Moonlight comes,
This reflected light,
To warm the eyes until dawn.
Will the moon and stars collide?
The sun approaches,
Yearning for the lips of morning,
Where she awaits.

The Truth

Her body, exposed and bare,
Radiant in its softness,
Adorned with intricate tattoos.
His fingers glide, tracing their lines,
Seeking the stories they conceal.

Each unique inked masterpiece
Whispers secrets untold.
He wonders, wants to know,
Will they unveil the depths
Of her passionate past?

In her eyes, mysteries reside,
Yet elusive, hard to read.
Her words, carefully chosen,
Reveal mere fragments
Of the mosaic she conceals.

She steers the conversation
To the realm of present delight,
Yearning to forge new memories.
But he persists, exploring further,
Will her art finally disclose the truth?

Inscribed upon her canvas
Lies a history of passion and pain.
The tapestry of her existence,

Woven with love and loss,
Experiences that shaped her soul.

With patient persistence,
He delves deeper into her depths,
Respecting the boundaries she sets,
Yet longing to understand.

The true masterpiece before him,
The truth, elusive and impactful,
Unfolds at its own pace.
As their connection deepens,
He knows, in time, her art
Will illuminate her hidden self.

Forbidden Whispers

As moonlight caresses the hidden night,
He enters my thoughts, a concealed delight.
Whispers in shadows, an enigmatic spell,
Our hearts intertwined, locked in a fervent embrace,
Fighting unexplainable feelings, love does find its place.

With stolen glances, a fire takes flight,
Passion ablaze, forbidden delight.
In its hidden depths, true beauty is discovered,
Bound by the chains of societal norms,
We dance on the brink where secrets take form.

No remorse we hold, solely desires untold,
In this newfound reality, our souls unfold.
For in the abyss of darkness, we've found light,
Forbidden whispers, secrets we'll confide,
In each stolen moment, our hearts collide.

So let the world judge, let them condemn,
Our love will endure, not break or bend.
In covert corners we dare to touch,
Did fate guide us down this treacherous trail?
A clandestine union, bound to prevail.

Unraveling Vows

Oh, until death do us part, they say,
A promise made on that fateful day.
But now we stand, worlds apart,
No love remains, just bitter hearts.

Once upon a time, we held hands,
Bound by passion's complex strands.
But time eroded our tender bliss,
Leaving behind an empty abyss.

We're no longer lovers, that much is clear,
The fire's extinguished, the end drawing near.
The laughter faded, the smiles grew thin,
Leaving behind a hollow din.

Oh, until death do us part, they decree,
But what about our own autonomy?
Must we suffer in silence, live in despair,
Merely because of a vow we once did swear?

The sarcasm lingers, a bitter taste,
As we navigate this loveless space.
Until death do us part, the words reside there,
A harsh reminder of a thrill now stripped bare.

But amidst the sorrow, we find our voice,
Choosing to live, to make our own choice.

For life is too short to be confined
By promises made, now far behind.

Oh, until death do us part, they preach,
But we'll define our own destiny, each.
Unshackled, we'll follow our own course,
Unswayed by others' opinions, without remorse.

Back in the Game

I close my eyes and think of the memories,
You are still there inside my mind,
But I won't cry over you now you are gone,
For I am in a good place and life moves on.
It is what it is, there is no "we,"
That is something I can clearly see.

Don't think I am in the dark and feeling blue,
Trust me, I am totally getting over you.
For here I am,
Back in the game, sharper and sharper each day,
Don't make the mistake to underestimate me,
I know very well how to play.

Swiping left and swiping right,
Who does not want to have some fun tonight?
Endless online chatting not allowed,
Because when I get bored, there is no road back.
This jungle is filled with predators and prey,
He who can't play with fire, get out of my way!

Searching for Batman:
A Sarcastic Single's Quest

Oh, the joys of being single at fifty,
With her sarcasm sharp and her wit so nifty.
In this grand quest for love, she must be picky,
For she needs a hero, her own dear Batman, swiftly.

No ordinary mortal will suffice,
She demands a caped crusader who is oh-so-nice.
A partner to rescue her from her solitary plight,
To bring adventure, thrill, and endless delight.

But alas, her requirements are truly rare,
Her checklist grows long, she drives men to despair.
He should scale rooftops, swing from the trees,
And solve riddles with ease, if he truly aims to please.

But where, oh where, does one find such a man?
Perhaps Gotham City, or a comic book fan?

A billionaire's fortune would be nice,
A Batmobile to chauffeur, would add some spice.
Gadgets and gizmos aplenty, in his utility belt,
To rescue her from boredom, her heart melted.

Yet here she is, still single and waiting,
Her hopes are high, but her prospects are deflating.
Perhaps she has set her standards too high,

Or maybe her Bat-signal was lost in the sky.

But fear not, for she jests and she teases,
Being single at fifty isn't all that it seems.
For life is full of wonders, she is so much more.

So, here's to being selective, sarcastic, and bold,
As we journey through life, our hearts unfold.
Love knows no limits, no matter how complex,
And perhaps, she'll find her very own Batman, who knows
what comes next.

Champions of Change

Unlocking the Power of Differences

Diversity, Equity, Inclusion—
The three inseparable pillars that make workplaces thrive.
Creating a space that is welcoming and free,
Where every employee can truly feel alive.

Diversity brings a range of experiences and views,
A vital ingredient for innovation and growth.
It broadens perspectives and sparks new ideas,
Creating a workplace that is vibrant and bold.

Equity ensures that every employee is treated the same,
Regardless of their background, ethnicity, or gender.
It creates a culture that is fair and just,
With equal opportunities that each one can embrace.

Inclusion is the final piece of this puzzle,
To create a culture where everyone belongs.
A space that is welcoming and safe,
To ensure that every employee can belong.

Together, these pillars create a workplace culture
That is diverse, equitable, and inclusive for all.
Where everyone can grow,
And their contributions can help the organization soar.

So let's embrace DEI with open hearts and minds,
Build a workplace culture that is truly sublime.

Where every employee can reach their full potential,
And drive the organization towards success.

A Flavorful World

Neurodiversity is a symphony of flavors,
Each brain is a unique instrument in the orchestra.
It celebrates differences in thought and perception,
A strength that adds depth and richness to life.

The neurodivergent may see the world through a different lens,
But it does not make them inferior, broken, or flawed.
Their distinct perspectives, insights, and talents
Can light up our world with innovation and creativity.

It is time to build a world that is inclusive and accepting,
Where conformity is not the norm and diversity is celebrated.
Not just tolerated, but embraced and understood,
Where everyone is valued for their ability to contribute.

We must learn to cherish our differences,
Create a world that is more compassionate and kind.
To be receptive to new ideas and ways of thinking,
Where everyone is valued for their skills and talents.

Let's break free from old patterns and embrace the new,
Welcome empathy, understanding, and so much more.
It's time to savor the variety that neurodiversity brings.

Can we create a world that is truly inclusive and flavorful?
A world that is ultimately beautiful!

Celebrating Unique Melodies

I am an advocate for inclusion,
A champion for every unique infusion.
Each mind deserves its own space
To shine brightly and find their pace.
For we are all special in our own way, that much is true,
And this is what makes us beautiful too.

I fight for a world where diversity reigns,
Where differences are celebrated,
Unique perspectives are elevated.
From autism to ADHD, dyslexia to OCD,
Each mind has its own melody,
A unique song, with its distinctive symphony.

Let's break down the walls of exclusion,
Truly embrace inclusion.
For every person, every mind,
Deserves a place in humankind.
For in our diversity, we find strength,
A world where everyone can go to any length.

Since inclusion is the key to our success,
We need to foster communities where everyone can progress.
My message is to build bridges, not walls.
We should embrace diversity in all its calls.
Please listen to the stories that need to be told,
So we can create a world where everyone can unfold.

Open Your Eyes to a World of Colors

I am an advocate for inclusion,
A champion in a world of colors, diverse and bright.
Autism whispers its unique light,
Through understanding's lens, we shall see
The beauty in minds, beautifully free.

Autism's voice, a symphony unique,
Unveiling perspectives we all must seek.
Together we stand, hand in hand,
United in love, we can truly understand.

Through patience and kindness, we can unfold
The treasures within, waiting to be told.
Let's shatter the barriers, break down the wall,
Embracing diversity, embracing all.

Women of Impact

Come together,
Let's continue to inspire
In our own communities and beyond.
Empower the women surrounding us,
Give them a helping hand.

We find connection
Showing vulnerability and authenticity.
It all depends on how
You approach life.
Just like a road has bumps,
A journey is never without challenge.

We all have experienced
Loss and pain,
But we also know how it feels
To be in love, loved by
Women of Impact.
Come together.

Let's be the catalysts for hope,
Unlocking potential,
Igniting the fire in others.
Be the guide for those
Who are still trying
To find their purpose.

Women of Impact,
Come together.
Share the stories,
The laughter.
But please…
Don't be afraid to show the tears.

Celebrating Cultural Diversity

Cultural diversity, what a wonder to behold,
A melting pot of knowledge, stories, and tales untold.
From the Netherlands to Dubai and so many other countries I have seen,
Different backgrounds, different experiences, different scenes.

Some may see it as a threat, a challenge to their way of life,
But that's just fear talking, drowning out the beauty and the strife.
For when we come together, we create something new and bright,
A world of innovation, ideas, and delight.

It's not just about the fun, though that's a part of it too,
Cultural diversity makes us stronger, more resilient, and true.
When we learn from each other, we develop empathy and care,
Breaking down the walls that divide us, making life a bit more fair.

So let's celebrate our differences, and let's do it with pride,
For we're all human beings, with hopes and dreams that coincide.
Whether you're Dutch, Emirati, or from any other place,
Let's embrace our uniqueness, and create a world of grace.

Symphony of Emiratisation

In the realm of transformation, where diversity holds sway,
I witnessed the power that lights up the workplace each day.
As a consultant, I beheld a symphony come alive,
Emiratisation's melody resounded, harmonious and thriving.

Imagine an orchestra, diverse in its grace,
Each instrument is unique, with its own vibrant pace.
Emiratis, the voices that rise with pride and might,
Their talents, their stories, a beacon shining bright.

No mere numbers or quotas, but inclusion's grand design,
An invitation to embrace, to intertwine.
For Emiratisation seeks unity's profound art,
To honor a culture's tapestry, a true work of heart.

Knowledge sharing blooms, as petals open wide,
Emirati insights, a treasure to confide.
Markets understood, community connections made,
Guiding decisions with wisdom's precious blade.

Cultural sensitivity, a bridge built with care,
Embracing traditions, values to hold and share.
A commitment to respect, a deep-rooted bond,
Fostering relationships, where trust can correspond.

Talent nurtured tenderly, with mentorship's embrace,
A transformative investment, real potential to chase.

For Emiratisation fuels dreams to take flight,
Building a future, empowered, shining bright.

Aspiring leaders emerge, role models bold and strong,
Inspiring generations, urging them to belong.
With Emirati success, a flame forever lit,
Motivating dreams, amplifying their grit.

Let us compose a masterpiece, a symphony so grand,
Where every instrument finds its rightful stand.
Embracing uniqueness, united we shall be,
A chorus of voices, celebrating unity.

So, let us strive together, each verse an invitation,
To create an inclusive workplace, a shining constellation.
In the journey of Emiratisation, let us take part,
And compose a symphony that resonates from heart to heart.

Riddle It

Let me introduce myself,
I represent endless possibilities.
You can achieve more with me
Then doing it on your own.

What am I?

Are you aware
That I come in many forms?
Think of a variety in age and generations,
In gender, ability, and so much more.

What am I?

I can only prosper
When coupled with Inclusion.
It is like the flower needs the rain,
Like the winter needs the spring.

What am I?

As a team, there is no challenge
That you and I can't overcome.
I reflect hope and inspiration,
Stand by my side.

What am I?

Be curious and learn about me.
I represent different ideas and views,
My background, my uniqueness,
Can truly help adding value.

What am I?

I ignite change and make it stick.
Don't push me back
Due to lack of knowledge.
Join hands with me instead.

What am I?

Together our lights burn longer
And so much brighter,
Higher and higher, no limits,
Until we reach the stars.

What am I?

Embrace the uniqueness of others.
Our time to shine has come.
It's all within our reach.

What am I?

I am Diversity.
That is me.

Shattering the Silence

In the jungle of thoughts, a battle unseen,
Where mental diseases hide, their presence keen.
Anxiety, a relentless beast, its grip so tight,
Leaving hearts racing, minds filled with fright.

The weight of worry, a constant companion,
Creating turmoil within.
Depression, a shadow that lingers and cloaks,
Draining colors from life, leaving hearts broken.

The heavy fog, the weight of despair,
This is my plea for understanding, for people to truly care.
Bipolar, a rollercoaster of emotions high and low,
A dance between euphoria and depths of woe.

The swinging pendulum, a challenge to endure,
I am seeking empathy, support that is pure.
Schizophrenia, a maze of altered perception,
Voices and visions, a complex intersection.

What is needed is compassion, to really see the person beyond,
There is so much more to understand.
Attention Deficit Hyperactivity Disorder, a mind on the run,
A symphony of distractions, battles to be won.

I am asking you for patience, for understanding's grace,
To nurture their strengths, to create an inclusive space.
Post-Traumatic Stress Disorder, scars unseen,
Triggered memories, haunting and often frightening.

This is my call for creating a safe environment,
To heal the wounded soul, to restore what once was.
Eating disorders, a distorted lens of self,
A fight against demons that whisper, that shout.
Let's foster body positivity, a culture of love,
To embrace every shape and size, not humiliate and criticize.
Borderline Personality Disorder, emotions like a storm,
A struggle to find stability.

A helping hand, give them a lifeline to extend,
To support their journey, to help them mend.
These are just glimpses, mere fragments of a whole,
Mental diseases that touch every heart and soul.

Let's break the stigma, erase judgment,
To create a world of understanding, where minds shine bright.
In unity, we can create a haven of compassion,
Education and awareness, the tools in our possession.

For mental health matters, it is time to ignite
A movement of acceptance, where every voice takes flight.
So let us walk hand in hand, with empathy as our guide,
Spreading awareness, erasing the divide.

Together, we can make a difference, create a space
Where mental diseases find solace, and hearts embrace.

Gender Equality

Every time there's a global crisis,
Our world can't be at risk
Of losing hard-fought equity gains.
Gender equality can be achieved.

If only everyone would walk the walk,
Instead of talking.
If not us, then who?
If not now, then when?

Together we can and should work
Towards a more gender-equal world.
On International Women's Day and beyond,
This should be a top priority.

If only everyone would walk the walk,
Instead of talking.
If not us, then who?
If not now, then when?

Don't let anybody tell you
That there are set paths for you to follow.
Don't give up on your dreams and passion.
When the world around us is shaken,
You are stronger than the storm.
I promise you,
You can be anything.

Some say women can never beat men,
But I don't want to race ahead of anyone.
Just stand beside me,
Be an ally, not a bystander.

If only everyone would walk the walk,
Instead of talking.
If not us, then who?
If not now, then when?

Gender inequality is so much part
Of the fabric of our society.
Why shouldn't we all be treated the same?
To have equal rights and equal pay.
Equality is not a privilege but a human right.

If we want to be successful,
We need to be on this journey all united.

Without gender equality today,
A sustainable and equal future
Remains beyond our reach.
Aren't we in this together?

If only everyone would walk the walk,
Instead of talking.
If not us, then who?
If not now, then when?

Echoes of War: A Cry for Peace

In the shadow of war's dark storm,
The bombs explode with deafening roar,
Leaving destruction in their wake,
And cities burning to the core.

The air is thick with smoke and ash,
The stench of sulfur fills the air,
And through it all, I cannot help but ask,
Why must we always fight and destroy?

If my voice means nothing to this world,
Then why do they seek to silence me?
If my words have no power to unfurl,
Then why do they seek to murder me?

Let's break the cycle, change the game,
And find a new way to coexist.
Where love and peace are not just a claim,
But a reality that can persist.

So let us rise up and take a stand,
Against the wars that tear us apart.
True healing and a better life await,
When we rise up and end this cycle of hate.

A Call to Conscience

In the depths of war's relentless grip,
Where innocence is crushed by chaos' whip,
Beneath the rubble, shattered dreams reside,
Orphans of war, their futures stolen,
And their hopes were denied.

Why must their tears be seen as mere dust,
As if their lives hold no sacred trust?
But let us not look the other way,
For in their faces, we see our shared kin,
The reminder of a world affected by sin.

To break this cycle, we must first believe
That compassion and love can truly achieve
A shift in consciousness, a turning tide,
Where empathy reigns and wounds can subside.

Let our actions speak louder than hollow words,
As we forge paths where peace and hope are heard.
Let's build a place for the orphans of war,
To heal the wounds and offer them a better space.

We should foster a world where love will preside,
Until the cries of pain are finally eased.

Just a Shadow

It all seems fine again for you
Till the next time.
The next time will come for sure,
Turning in violence upon you.
You are hiding in your little world,
Can't you see?
You need to escape,
Have the courage to run.

My dear friend, habibti,
You are just a shadow of the woman you could be,
Like a hidden oasis in the desert that the world will never see.
You have no thoughts for tomorrow, only the confusion of
today,
And it feels like hell.

All these promises that it will never happen again,
What do you believe?
That feeling you have,
What to do,
When your back is against the wall?
Hurtful words have left their scars,
And still you can't leave.
Things will change, won't they?

My dear friend, habibti,
You are just a shadow of the woman you could be,

Like a hidden oasis in the desert that the world will never see.
You have no thoughts for tomorrow, only the confusion of today,
And it feels like hell.

Love should not hurt.
You should be happy.
Love should not be conditional.
You should feel great.
Love should not break you.
You should be you.

My dear friend, habibti,
You are just a shadow of the woman you could be,
Like a hidden oasis in the desert that the world will never see.
You have no thoughts for tomorrow, only the confusion of
today,
And it feels like hell.

Please don't lose yourself for too long
That you forget what it is like
To be you,
The beautiful woman, the wonderful friend you are.
My dear friend, habibti,
Isn't it time to rise?

Bittersweet Memory

Ignite the flames, let the past be the past.
No future awaits, it's time to move on.
Some things are transient, destined to fade.

Sweep away the ashes, leave no trace behind.
Close the door on what once was,
Ensure it's gone, no remnants to find.

No room for regret, no more tears to shed.
What's done is done, the chapters close.
Time passes, transforming into years ahead.

Wasn't it evident from the very start
This love was never meant to thrive?
Yet why does a dagger still pierce my heart?

Promise, never return to my side.
All that lingers of our shared past,
A single bittersweet memory shall reside.

Lost and Confused

I sometimes still think
It is only a dream.
How can this be real?
I am really hurt;
It is how I feel.
Bittersweet memories keep coming back,
And so do the tears.
I hear your voice,
But as quick as the smile comes,
It just disappears in a split second.
I can't explain your behavior.
Wasn't I always there for you?

Lost and confused,
All the things you did not say,
Emotions and feelings kept to yourself.
I was like a boomerang;
You threw me over and over again.
Only every time you threw me,
I always seemed to come back,
Back to you, back to pain.
Whatever I tried to do,
Nothing was right for you.
Now I can finally find my way.

It is hard to deal with all of this.
I just don't know where to start.
I guess that is what happens
When someone breaks your heart.
My friends see I am struggling,
How I try to smile through my tears.
They don't know I am crying
When I am home, all alone.
Because I do feel lost and confused,
And deep down I wish
You have these feelings too.

Come Out and Play

When exactly did you forget
About your inner child?
Why taking life so seriously,
No more time for silly things?
Where are the crazy adventures?

Don't you realize
That the world is our playground?
When did you stop having fun?

Reach out and take my hand,
I will show you the way.

You Don't Know

You talk about love
And how you miss me.

Don't waste my time.
I am not a fool.
It has always been about you,
Hell to "You and I."

I doubt if you know
What it means to really
Crave someone
During these sleepless nights,
Tossing and turning,
All by yourself.

To feel incomplete,
As if you lost a body part,
Still trying to touch it,
Only to find out
It is no longer present.
How to become whole again?

To walk in the pouring rain,
Tears running down your cheeks,
Drowning in emotions
So intense,
Realizing there is
No happily ever after.

You talk about the future
And how we can be together.

Don't waste my time.
I am not a fool.
It has always been about you,
Hell to "You and I."

Eternal Love

Remember me when I am gone,
Gone far away to another place,
Where you can no longer look into my eyes,
No longer hold my hand,
Nor can I passionately return your kiss.
Please remember me and what we once had.

It is ok if you should forget me for a while,
And do not grieve.
If the memories should return,
Once the darkness has faded
And your sorrow is no longer there,
Better you forget and smile,
Instead of remembering and being sad.

Damn Those Eyes

If eyes are really the mirror of the soul,
It scares me,
Looking into yours.
I can almost feel your pain,
The things you are not telling me.

Do you think I can't see
How something is tearing you apart?
Let me hold you close,
Your skin pressed against me tight,
My body is telling you it will be alright.

Comfortably numb, you cannot speak,
So you leave to smoke a cigarette,
Too afraid to show your vulnerability.

Damn those eyes,
Eyes don't lie, words may try.
I wish I could make it better for you,
I know I can't.

You're your own cure.
There are ways to break this vicious cycle
Of negative thoughts.
Believe in yourself.
A bright shining light will illuminate your path.

Grief's Unspoken Verse

In the depths of sorrow's embrace,
Where silence lingers, an empty void,
A heart, heavy with the weight of grief,
Whispers words it cannot find, seeking relief.

When words fail to capture the essence
Of a love that defies all bounds,
Grief, a tempest that engulfs the soul,
Leaving scars unseen, yet taking its toll.

In the empty spaces between spoken lines,
We find echoes of a love that forever shines.
When words fail, the heart's language takes flight,
Through tears that flow, in the silence of night.

Though the emptiness may seem vast and wide,
Love transcends, it cannot be denied.
In the tender touch of a gentle breeze,
The warmth of sun rays, dancing on tranquil seas.

So let the tears fall, let the silence speak,
In the absence of words, love finds its peak.
For in the bittersweet journey of grief's tale,
We find comfort, when words fail.

Fragments of My Soul

Embracing Shadows

In shadows deep where darkness thrives,
Where sorrow weaves its haunting guise,
There lies a truth we often miss,
A whispered comfort, a gentle kiss.

For in this world of highs and lows,
Where joys may fade and troubles grow,
Remember well, amidst the fray,
It's okay, my friend, not to be okay.

In moments lost, when tears descend,
When shattered dreams refuse to mend,
Know that your heart can find its way,
Embracing the truth, it's okay not to be okay.

In vulnerability, strength resides,
A sanctuary where healing abides.
For struggles faced, a common thread,
No shame in seeking comfort instead.

The weight you carry, burdens untold,
In restless nights, your spirit bold.
Find solace in the night's ballet,
It's okay, my friend, not to be okay.

Through silent battles waged within,
Where shattered pieces dance and spin,

Reach out your hand, let others say,
"It's okay, my friend, not to be okay."

For in the tapestry of human grace,
Each thread of pain finds its rightful place.
And from the darkness, seeds shall sow,
A garden of hope, where strength can grow.

So if the storms inside persist,
Remember this, amidst the mist,
You are not alone along this way,
It's okay, my friend, not to be okay.

Let tenderness embrace your fears,
And wipe away the silent tears.
For in your struggle, strength will bloom,
Revealing beauty beyond the gloom.

Within life's mosaic of light and shade,
Amidst the chaos where melodies cascade,
Hold on tight, through every ebb and sway,
It's okay, my friend, not to be okay.

Echoes of Alteration

Old woman, poor woman,
My heart is bleeding.
Who or what is to blame?
You cannot go through life
Without going through hardship.
I know you had your fair share.

Old woman, poor woman,
The darkness in your head
Was disturbing you, confusing you.
I can't help but wonder now,
To whom did these voices belong?
Who did you see when you looked in the mirror?
A stranger, someone new every day?

Old woman, poor woman,
Mother, my mother.
I realize now you are gone,
That it was not you talking.
It makes me sad.
How can I describe my feelings with the right words?
Yes, it hurts like hell.

The Flight to Freedom

As I awaken each day,
A restlessness grips my soul.
I feel trapped in a cage,
My wings clipped and incomplete.

I am meant to soar high,
A free bird with boundless reach.
But something holds me back,
A force that keeps me chained.

If only you were here
To hold me without touch,
To keep me without chains,
And set my spirit free.

Like the Phoenix,
I will rise from the ashes of my past,
Renewed and unafraid,
Ready to spread my wings and fly.

So let me burn and be reborn,
A symbol of endless change.
With newfound strength and courage,
I will soar to great heights again.

Dementia's Toll

Aged, weathered soul,
My heart weeps in sorrow,
Feeling the weight of his confusion,
Relentlessly chasing him, day by day.

Once, the world bowed at his command,
Now a stranger stares back from the mirror,
Whispers of thoughts occasionally heard,
"Oh God, can that truly be me?"

Yet darkness prevails more often,
Unleashing anguished screams,
A gradual descent into dementia's embrace,
Leaving behind a mere shadow of his past.

Gone, the magnificence, strength, and intellect,
That once defined this noble man,
Yet amidst the fading remnants,
Love and compassion still hold their ground.

In the gentle touch and patient embrace,
We find solace and connection,
Amidst the fragments of memory,
A testament to his enduring spirit.

So let us cherish each fleeting moment,
Embrace the time we still have together,

For within the depths of his fading mind,
A lifetime of stories, love, and resilience remain.

Shadows of Love

Stay by my side, my love,
I can't bear to let you go.
In this dimly lit room,
Your heartbeat grows faint and low.

I yearn to dispel this darkness,
To bring back the light we knew.
Can we reclaim what we once had?
Oh, if only this were a bad dream.

I pinch myself, hoping to awaken,
To escape this painful reality.
But the truth is what I seek,
No more lies, no more duality.

My love, my soulmate, speak,
Why must we face such despair?
Tell me, for I need to know,
What burden makes you feel you must disappear?

Yesterday's sorrows won't fade,
But can we forge a brighter tomorrow?
Can we find the strength to save ourselves?
To find peace in the midst of this sorrow?

Together, let's seek the light,
Amidst the darkness that surrounds us.

For in our unity and if we really fight,
Hope and healing can be found.

In Loving Memory

My dearest butterfly,
It has been years since you flew away,
Yet your face remains etched in my mind,
As if you never left, but chose to stay.
Life can be so unfair,
Some things we cannot change or repair.
Please know that you will always be loved,
Memories don't fade or dissolve.

My dearest butterfly,
It has been years since you passed,
But your laughter still echoes in my heart,
As if it never stopped or crashed.
Life can be so harsh,
Taking away those we hold dear.
I will always cherish our moments together,
Keep your memory forever near.

My dearest butterfly,
It has been years since you departed,
But the scent of your perfume lingers still,
As if you never truly parted.
Life can be so tough,
Bringing pain that cuts deep and rough.
I will always be grateful for what you taught me,
How you inspired me to be.

My dearest butterfly,
Oh, how I miss you so much,
I wish I could hug you just one more time,
Feel your warmth, your love, your touch.
But until we meet again,
I will hold onto the memories we made,
Keep you close in my heart,
Where your love and light will never fade.

Tangled Deceptions

A whirlpool of feelings swirl within,
Sadness and anger intertwine,
Emotions overflow, a torrent unleashed,
In this intricate web of lies.

What drives souls to lead dual lives?
To wear masks and put on disguises,
When even your name is but a facade.
Did the mundane lack allure?

Craving perpetual thrills,
An insatiable hunger, never quenched,
Truth obscured, hidden away,
In the labyrinth of your deceit.

Were any fragments genuine at all?
I ponder, my heart heavy with doubt,
Or were they all mere illusions,
Born from the depths of your imagination?

Did you deceive even yourself,
Believing the tales you spun,
As laughter echoed, shisha smoke twirled in the air,
And lips met in fleeting connection.

Were we ever truly friends,
Or casualties of your elaborate charade?

Lost in the maze of your tangled web,
A tapestry woven with deceit's embrace?

I question the authenticity of it all,
When did falsehoods blend with reality?
Did you even believe your own illusions,
As we laughed, smoked, and kissed?

And now, you depart from this stage,
But even in death, uncertainty lingers.
Did you truly perish or live anew,
In another narrative of your design?

Memories Don't Die

When the day comes
Where words no longer
Flow from my heart,
Don't look for me.
I will be gone.

When the day comes
Where passion has been
Replaced by routine,
Don't try to cage me.
Birds need to be free.

When the day comes
Where what's lost weighs
Heavier than what still remains,
Don't be sad.
Our memories will last.

Letting Go

Two simple words, yet profound—
I never knew their weight before.
In your presence, I have found
Their true meaning, deep at the core.

Because of you, I comprehend
The essence of letting go's embrace.
Our moments together, I intend
To cherish, within time and space.

With utmost effort, I strive
To hold dear what we have shared,
But now, it's time for me to thrive,
To release what can't be repaired.

These two words, like a gentle breeze,
Guide me on a path of growth.
As I embrace the art of letting go,
A new clarity unfolds.

In this journey of discovery,
Because of you, I've come to see
That letting go is the key,
To find myself and be free.

Ebb and Flow

Within the depths, I am drowning,
Struggling against life's relentless current.
Silent battles, concealed from the world's gaze,
While I dance and wear a mask of mirth.

Outwardly, laughter spills from my lips,
Unaware of the tears seeping within.
Crashing waves surround me with their might,
Yet I stand tall, defying their tumultuous din.

It takes a forceful wave to shatter me,
To send me tumbling into the abyss,
And I surrender, yielding to its power,
Lost in the depths, engulfed by its kiss.

In these deep waters, I am trapped,
Awaiting the return of a guiding light.
Hope flickers, its warmth a distant flame,
Trying to reclaim my place with all my might.

How I long for a gentle embrace,
To be lifted back onto stable ground,
To refocus on what truly holds meaning,
And leave behind life's shallow surroundings.

Within the ebb and flow of despair's embrace,
Hope's gentle current beckons to be held,

Guiding me to shores where I belong,
Reviving my spirit with a radiant grace.

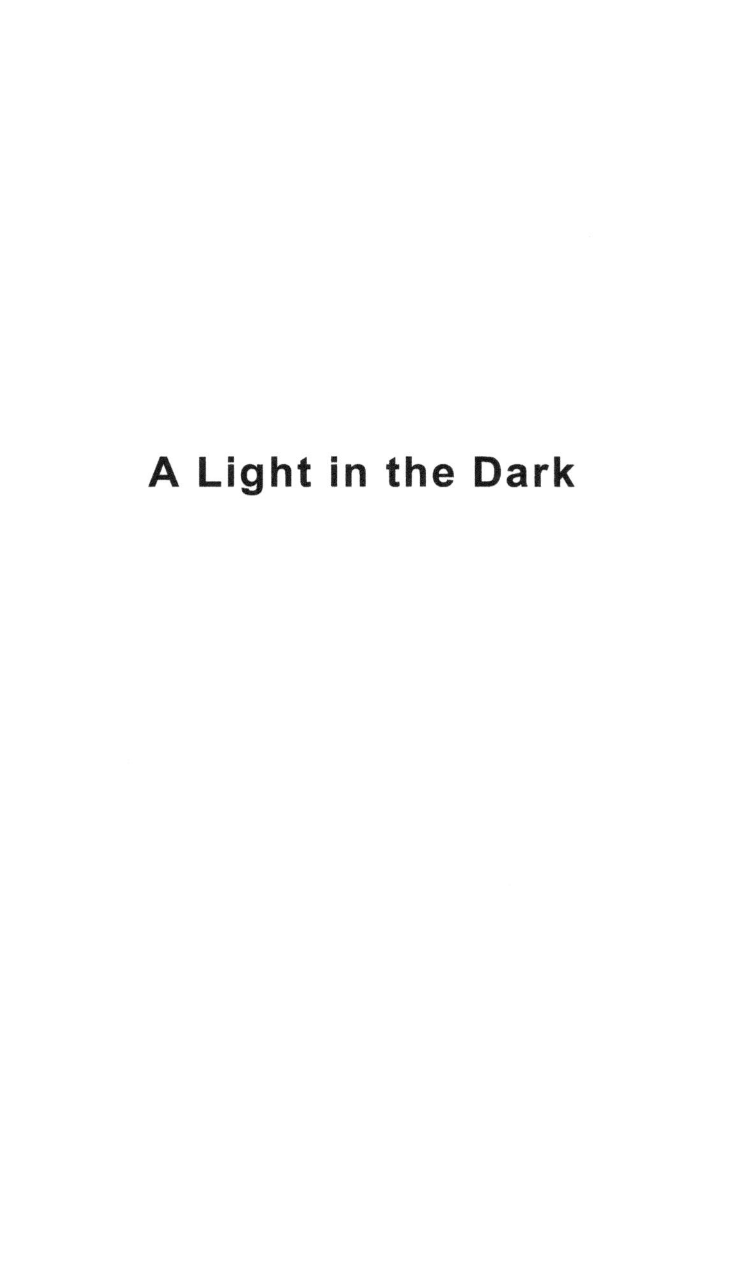

A Light in the Dark

Menopause Mischief

In midlife's whimsical haze, a tale unfolds
Of a woman, fifty and quite bold.
Menopause is playing tricks on her, life becomes a maze,
Sometimes even a complete mischief, a bewildering phase.

Sleep evades her like a fleeting dream,
Hormonal chaos, oh, to the extremes!
Joints can creak and groan with each move,
Her belly is bloated, her pants disapprove.

But she tries to face it all with a hearty laugh,
Menopause's tricks can't dampen her chaff.
With humor as her armor, she stands tall,
A warrior in the battlefield, she will conquer it all.

In this age of change, she is finding her way,
Menopause mischief, she'll conquer day by day.
For laughter, her secret, is keeping her sane,
A reminder that life's quirks hold no chain.

Becoming Beacons of Hope and Light

Living my life in the Western sphere,
What did I know of the Islamic culture?
Of their beliefs and their holy days?
The true spirit of Ramadan was a mystery.
My eyes were blind, my mind was closed,
To traditions so far from what I had been exposed to.

But then I learned of Eid al-Fitr,
The celebration that marks the end of the holy month.
I started to see the beauty of the Muslim tradition,
With all the values it instills.

In a world that often divides,
Eid al-Fitr is a reminder to set aside our differences,
A time to focus on what unites,
Not on what tears us apart.
That is my message to the world.
I believe in our shared humanity.

While I may not practice the same religion,
I know that I can learn from Eid al-Fitr,
For the message of compassion and forgiveness
Is universal, as it transcends barriers.

May Eid al-Fitr be a time to renew,
A time to remember the deeper way,

A commitment to peace and love
Will bring us closer to unity.

By working together towards a better society,
We can make a positive difference,
Beacons of hope, beacons of light,
That is what we can be.

The True Spirit of Ramadan

What did I know about Ramadan
Growing up, working, and living my life in the West?
My friends and I did not differ too much.
We shared similar backgrounds and beliefs, the same
ethnicity.
How could I understand the true spirit of the holy month
When my eyes were blind and my mind was closed to
traditions
So far apart from what I was taught and was familiar to me?

A lot can change in 7 years.
Showing curiosity and a genuine interest in other cultures
Has brought me new friends, diverse in so many aspects.
The UAE is where I want to be, my home, with over 200
nationalities.
This country represents a combination of tolerance and
harmony.
Respect and acceptance of others
Are deep-rooted values in our community.

Ramadan is not about being thirsty and hungry.
Not about craving a cigarette or shisha.
Ramadan is not about forbidding hugs, kisses, and sex.
From the early hours of dawn till the hours of dusk.
It is not about the sumptuous buffets for Iftar.
The real purpose of fasting is to show righteousness.
To be thankful for the gift of health and for what you have.

Ramadan is about being good to others.
Inviting them at your table
For a meal of kindness, a glass filled with hope.
A bowl full of love and a spoonful of laughs.
Ramadan is about helping those who are in need.
It is about removing the pain of offense from your heart.
To open the door of forgiveness and to feed your soul.

That for me is the true spirit of Ramadan.
Ramadan Mubarak.

This is Life

"My friend,

We all have our own storms and trials.
Life is full of ups and downs.
Enjoy the ups to their fullest.
Have courage during the downs,
As they won't last forever.

It can take time to find new paths.
No one said it would be easy.
Hang in there, my friend.
I believe in you.
You will overcome it.

When you are losing hope,
Remember you sometimes have to
fight through the bad days
To earn the best days of your life.
We have all been there.
You are not alone.

When you can only feel the darkness,
Please don't be afraid
To notice the beauty around you.
The tide will turn.
It always does.
You are not alone.

When your head is full of worries,
Feeding off your precious energy,
Please don't be afraid
To ignore the demons.
Your own voice is stronger than that.
You are not alone.

When the sun starts shining again,
Amazing things will happen.
Please don't be afraid
To turn your face toward the light
And let the sun rays ignite your fire again.
You are not alone.

Hang in there, my friend.
I believe in you.
You will overcome it."

Finding Myself Again

Listen,
A thunderstorm in my head.
Lightning crashes,
Can I hide?
Keep me safe.
This will pass again.
It always does.

Look up,
A shimmering light.
Can I run?
Take my hand,
Lead me through the shadows,
This valley of dark emotions.

Feel,
The wind touches my face.
Sun rays gently caress my skin.
Can I dance?
Oh, beautiful life,
Thank you for this lesson.
It is time to be whole again.

It Is What It Is

There are days when I am
An adventurous soul,
Eager to conquer the world.
Other days, I become the wild,
Crazy one,
Always seeking spontaneity.
And on certain days,
Emotions overwhelm,
Leaving me at a loss for words.

Most days, I embody
A fusion of all these facets,
Like a uniquely crafted cocktail.
But no day passes by
Without my endeavor
To seize the best life offers.

Once Upon a Time

As time drifts by with ease,
My mind begins its game,
Deceiving my senses.
Only now do I grasp
The truth of my actions.
I painted a flawless scene—
You and I,
Bound for eternal bliss.

Cease the dreaming!
Life's tale is not enchanted.
Frogs remain mere frogs.
Yet, even if they transformed,
I know the truth well:
Restlessness would consume us,
Longing for new escapades.
Now, unfurl your wings,
Ignite your passions once more,
And embrace the fervent flames.

Women at the Forefront

Women's empowerment is so much more
It is not a catchy slogan.
I truly believe that when women succeed,
Everyone benefits.

I have a vision
Where we as women at the forefront
Will continue to inspire others
In our own communities and beyond,
To believe in their passion and purpose.
Where we will learn from each other's culture,
Bridge the gaps, and overcome the challenges.
We will ensure that needs are voiced.

I have a vision
Where we as women at the forefront
Can be the role models
For those who might lack access
To support networks,
Who need champions
To help progress their careers.
Collaboration at its best.
We, women at the forefront,
Let's give birth to innovative ideas,
Nurture an environment
Of synergy and satisfaction.
We lead, we make decisions, we impact.

We, women at the forefront,
Need to be the change we want to see,
Empowering other women,
Give them a helping hand.
Together we make it happen.
Together we thrive.

A Vision for Tomorrow

Let us envision a better tomorrow,
Kindness and understanding light the way,
Where divisions crumble and unity thrives,
Resolving conflicts, as hope survives.

Let nature's voice be heard
To heal the wounds of Earth's sacred ground,
Embracing sustainability, we pave the way
For generations to come.

May the shadows of poverty fade away
With equal opportunities,
Where the rights of all, both big and small,
Are protected and followed.

In this better tomorrow, let justice prevail
With fairness and integrity,
Empowering voices that have long been unheard,
And breaking the chains of some parts of this world.

With courage as our compass, we shall rise
Against injustice and prejudice,
For the dreams we hope to see come true
Lies the essence of a better tomorrow.

The Phoenix Within

The legendary Phoenix, a symbol of rebirth,
Teaches us the essence of our own true worth.
From the ashes it rises, in majestic flight,
A testament to resilience, burning bright.
With wings outstretched, it soars to the sky,
Defying limitations, aiming high.

In its fiery gaze, we find a reflection
Of the power we possess.
For within our hearts, an ember glows,
A spark of authenticity, only we can expose.
Embrace the flames, let pretenses fade,
Strip away the masks, don't be afraid.

Like the Phoenix, rise from the depths within,
Embrace your uniqueness, let your spirit truly sing.
No need for imitation or a borrowed guise,
Embrace your authenticity, a priceless prize.
So spread your wings, let your colors unfurl,
Be the most authentic version of yourself.

About the Author

Kirsten Westholter, Senior Culture and Leadership Transformation Advisor, is driven by an unwavering dedication to providing exceptional solutions that help businesses overcome their toughest challenges. Her passion extends beyond the world of business, as she fervently advocates for the creation of positive and inclusive business cultures, championing Diversity, Equity, and Inclusion (DE&I) at every opportunity. However, when Kirsten takes a break from the demanding world of slaying business challenges, she finds solace and creative expression in the written word.

Originally hailing from The Netherlands, Kirsten embarked on a transformative journey in 2016, leaving behind the comfort and predictability of her life in Amsterdam to embrace the vibrant landscapes of the United Arab Emirates. Since then, she has made it her mission to inspire others to step outside their comfort zones, ignite their inner fires, and fearlessly follow their hearts. Guided by her life motto, "Die with memories, not dreams," Kirsten encourages others to seize every moment and make the most of their existence.

Drawing from her own life experiences, Kirsten has truly embraced the legendary Phoenix as a symbol of resilience and rebirth. It is under the pseudonym Dubai Phoenix that she pours her heart and soul into her poetry, firmly believing that, no matter what challenges we face, we always possess the power to rise from the ashes and embrace transformation.

Kirsten's poems serve as poignant reflections of her personal journey and keen observations of the world around her. Through her words, she delves into the depths of love and emotions in their broadest sense, exploring the complexities of loss, and occasionally drawing striking parallels to the transformative journey of the Phoenix.